Accelerated Learning Mastery:

Learn Powerful Accelerated Learning Techniques to Instantly Boost your Ability to Learn & Remember Any Topic for Academic, Work & Business Success

Steve Chambers

© **Copyright 2018 by Steve Chambers - All rights reserved.**

The contents of this book may not be reproduced, duplicated or transmitted without direct written permission from the author.

Under no circumstances will any legal responsibility or blame be held against the publisher for any reparation, damages, or monetary loss due to the information herein, either directly or indirectly.

Legal Notice:

This book is copyright protected. This is only for personal use. You cannot amend, distribute, sell, use, quote or paraphrase any part or the content within this book without the consent of the author.

Disclaimer Notice:

Please note the information contained within this document is for educational and entertainment purposes only. Every attempt has been made to provide accurate, up to date and reliable complete information. No warranties of any kind are expressed or implied. Readers acknowledge that the author is not engaging in the rendering of legal, financial, medical or professional advice. The content of this book has been derived from various sources. Please consult a licensed professional before attempting any techniques outlined in this book.

By reading this document, the reader agrees that under no circumstances are is the author responsible for any losses, direct or indirect, which are incurred as a result of the use of information contained within this document, including, but not limited to, —errors, omissions, or inaccuracies.

Table of Contents

Introduction

Chapter 1: Getting Started with Accelerated Learning

Chapter 2: Setting Up a Better Learning Environment

Chapter 3: How to Make Learning Second Nature to You

Chapter 4: How to Dramatically Improve your Study Habits

Chapter 5: How to Boost your Focus to Laser Precision Levels

Chapter 6: Easy Techniques to Remember Facts and Figures – Fast

Chapter 7: Strategies for Better Listening

Chapter 8: Write and Retain – Better Note Taking

Chapter 9: How to Achieve Superb Reading Comprehension

Chapter 10: Boost your Learning with Mathematics

Chapter 11: How to Avoid Learning Mistakes

Bonus Chapter: Go-To Learning Strategies to Prepare for an Exam

Conclusion

What This Book Will Teach You

Are you curious to learn about Accelerated Learning but unsure where to start?

Have you always wanted to learn a topic or skill better and faster, but end up frustrated and barely learning anything at all?

If these questions relate well with you, then this book is for you. In this book you will find the basic essentials to learning Accelerated Learning. This book introduces readers to Accelerated Learning, the in's and out, the various processes and steps involved.

Who this Book is for

This book contains information on how to learn Accelerated Learning from a beginner level.

Readers who can benefit the most from the book include:

- Students who would like to know more about the Accelerated Learning as a skill to use in their studies and helping them learn better to produce better grades and higher scores on their exams.

- Working professionals interested in learning Accelerated Learning to help boost their ability to learn work-related skills for career advancement.

- Entrepreneurs who want to learn Accelerated Learning as another important skill to succeed on their business.

How this Book is Organized

This book is organized into three parts. The parts are best read in chronological order. Once you become familiar with all the steps outlined in the book, you can go directly to the techniques which apply to your current situation the best.

The three parts of the book are:

Part One outlines the essential topics on Accelerated Learning; how to get started the right way. The section also talks about how important it is to setup a better learning environment, as well as how to approach learning in general so that it becomes second nature to you.

Part Two is about Accelerated Learning in more detail. You'll learn how to dramatically improve study habits, become more focused on learning things and techniques to learn facts and figures better.

Part Three expands on previous chapters and features more Accelerated Learning techniques such as how to improve reading comprehension, getting better at Math and avoiding learning mistakes. Plus, a BONUS Chapter on how to prepare for an exam using effective strategies.

Introduction

Accelerating your learning process will not only benefit you as a student, it will drastically improve your life.

We can't help but learn as a species, but when we're young, we typically try to learn because that is what we're expected to do. We want to go out into the world and be independent and think for ourselves. But when we truly commit to accelerating our learning process while we're still young, what happens is that we end up building the life of our dreams. There is nothing we cannot learn, and there never is any limit to how much we can learn about the world around us.

However, there are those of us whose life circumstances haven't allowed us to maximize our learning experience. We get to a certain point in life, and we want to do something about this. We finally get down to work and get serious about our life. It's these people whom this book is especially meant for. Nothing is more exciting than watching an adult discover the vast potential inside themselves that never was demonstrated to them when they were a child.

These adults are driven like no other to be all that they can be. It is none other than life experience that has so wonderfully parented them to the point of so greatly accelerating their learning and life.

Only in recent years have we as a society finally discovered how incredible our brains are. Not that long ago, it was believed that adults could not learn. If you didn't learn as a child, it was believed that it was too late to start. Adult brains were considered to be unchangeable… like cement or brick.

How could we ever have thought such a thing?!

No matter what our age, there is no end to what we can learn. We keep our brains healthy by learning as much as we can at all times. It's never too late, either. All brains – no matter their condition – improve in the accelerated learning process.

So, get your brain ready to learn and learn some more!

Let's not forget in our accelerated learning process to study what foods to eat and what ways to exercise. Healthy brains require lots of blood flow that the only exercise provides and so many nutrients, minerals and fats that only organic vegetables, nuts, seeds and the highest quality proteins yield.

Our accelerated learning process will be invigorated by approaching our brain health from such a holistic point of view.

Congratulations on committing to your accelerated learning process by purchasing this book. I hope you enjoy all the many suggestions herein that will supercharge your brain and your life.

Chapter 1: Getting Started with Accelerated Learning

Chapter 1: Getting Started with Accelerated Learning

1.1

To begin the accelerated learning process, it is important to first understand your brain. No accelerated learning technique could have ever been developed without the study of the brain and how it works.

As we evolved, our brain evolved and, as the result, our one brain consists of 3 sub-brains: the brain stem, limbic system, and neocortex.

Our brainstem is responsible for our survival. Even reptiles have this part of the brain in common with us, explaining why it is often referred to as the reptilian brain. The brainstem regulates all the automatic functions in our bodies such as our heartbeat and breathing.

In terms of accelerated learning, we are most interested in the "fight or flight" aspect of the reptilian brain. Whenever we feel scared and/or threatened, this part of our brain totally shuts down all other parts of the brain so that we cannot think. Adrenaline kicks in and courses throughout our body to immediately put us into active survival mode.

This is the part of the brain that saved the lives of our ancestors whenever a predator attempted to hunt them down. However, it is this same part of our brain that automatically shuts down the rational part of our brain whenever we experience stress, fear, anxiety or feel threatened in any way. This is why stress reduction is so very important in the accelerated learning process.

The limbic system is the part of your brain that is sometimes referred to as the mammalian brain. As this term indicates, it is this part of our brain that we have in common with all other mammals. Our emotions, sex, immunity, and hormones are all controlled by this part of our brain.

Long-term memory is also controlled by the limbic system, and it is our brain's hippocampus, thalamus, and amygdala that are key to the accelerated learning process.

It is the amygdala that is responsible for evaluating whether a "fight or flight" is necessary. If the amygdala ever detects stress of any kind, it will automatically activate the brain stem and shut down the limbic system in response. This is why it is imperative that you have a system in place to manage all stress. The last thing that you want in the accelerated thinking process is for your amygdala to send everything down the tubes to your brain stem. Why? Because until you can convince your brain stem that no valid threat exists, you will not be able to think or learn.

The thalamus is the switchboard of our brain. It receives all the information from our senses and then sends it to the appropriate parts of our brain for processing. There are 2 primary directions all information is sent. The low road leads to the amygdala, and we already know what happens when information goes there. The high road leads to the sensory cortices: the place we want such information to go, instead.

These sensory cortices are located in our neocortex, directly above our hippocampus. It is the neocortex that makes us human. Our reason, thinking, language and abstract thinking are all possible thanks to the neocortex. Contained within the neocortex are the visual cortex, auditory cortex, and somatosensory cortex – the specific areas of our brain that are crucial to accelerated learning.

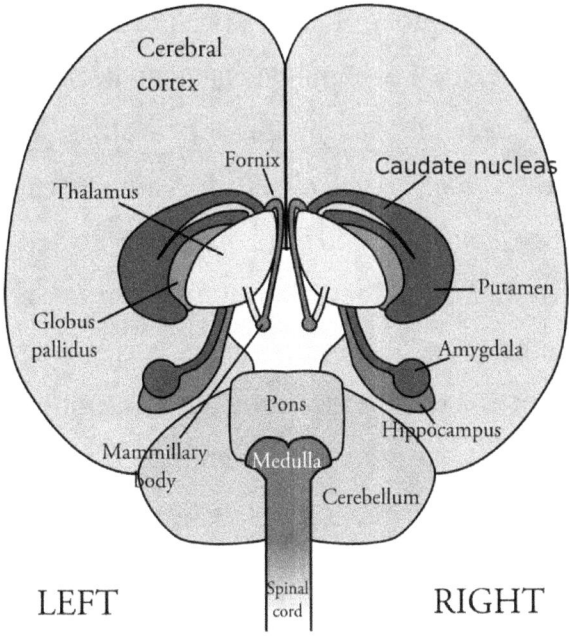

1.2

All incoming information from the thalamus is processed by all parts of the neocortex and then sent along to the prefrontal cortex. This is the part of our brain where working memory lives. If the prefrontal cortex determines that information should be stored in long-term memory, it is sent back to the cortex that originally processed it, thus, all visual long-term memory is stored in the visual cortex, all auditory long-term memory is stored in the auditory cortex and all kinesthetic long-term memory is stored in the somatosensory cortex. It is for this reason that activating as many senses as possible – visual, audial, kinesthetic and even taste and smell – when learning something will cause it to be more deeply ingrained in our brain.

Each of our brains has about 100 billion neurons – nerve cells – that connect with each other to form a vast network inside our brain. This is what makes thinking possible. Each neuron can connect with up to 20,000 other neurons which each connect with up to another 20,000 neurons and so on and so on. Really, truly, this is how each and every one of us is literally microcosms of the entire universe.

Neurons communicate with each other by way of electrical signals that can be referred to as brain waves. The four different kinds of brain waves are delta, theta, alpha, and beta.

The slowest brain wave is the delta. It is when we are asleep that we are in a delta. It is while we sleep that our body repairs itself, explaining why sleep is so very important to our health and, thus, our accelerated learning process.

The next step up from delta is theta. Faster than delta, the theta state is when we are falling asleep or in deep relaxation. When a person meditates, this is the brainwave they can activate. Theta enables the processing and storing of memories, explaining why it is so important to the accelerated learning process to have some kind of deep relaxation or meditation routine in place to manage all stress.

The fastest brain waves are beta which we experience in normal, everyday life. In beta, we are able to shift focus from one thing to another. Although this is the way that we get things done, it is not the best brain state for learning.

It is alpha that is the best for learning. In alpha, you are awake but relaxed. It is when our brain is at its most efficient. Any person who feels "in the zone" is in alpha state. Deep focus is what is possible in alpha, and this is where we want to be when in the accelerated learning process.

1.3

Thus, to accelerate our learning process, we need to keep the function of our brain in mind. To learn best, we need to be in a relaxed but alert state: alpha. When we get stressed, we immediately plunge into survival mode which downgrades us to hyper beta. We need to be calm to be able to most effectively process all the information that comes our way.

If you want to make sure you remember something, review it at bedtime. That way you'll go into theta when you're falling asleep, guaranteeing that your brain will fully process and store the information you just reviewed.

Involve as many senses as possible to maximize the learning process. A trick of the trade is to chew a certain brand and flavor of gum when you're learning something. Then when you chew that exact, same brand and flavor of gum again, your brain will be triggered to remember more of what you learned.

Remember, learning is a lot of what makes us human. So, it is the most natural thing in the world for every one of us to do. When we truly understand this point, we can settle down and not be so anxious about learning – not to mention accelerated learning. No matter what you think your level of knowledge or experience is, you can learn more than you know right now and there is zero limit to how much you can learn. It is only stress that limits how much you can learn, not your IQ. Remember that!

So, relax and decide what it is that you want to learn. Do you want to learn to program? Do you want to learn to speak Spanish? If so, what do you want to do with that knowledge? A good goal would be to write a computer program that will do something specific that you have in mind. Or to go to a party at the house of your friend from Mexico and speak only in Spanish. In the process of achieving such a concrete goal in real life, you will acquire so many new skills that you wouldn't have if you didn't have such a concrete goal to shoot for.

Research is important, but don't get stuck in research mode, or you won't ever achieve your goal. To truly learn, you actually have to go out into the world and do it. This is the last thing you typically want to do when you're still learning a skill, but you will never learn it and retain it if you skip this step as most people do. And this most likely will cause you to abandon your goal.

So, before going to that party, listen to and speak Spanish as much as you can. Use flashcards and speak the words aloud. Listen to audio recordings of others speaking the language and respond back in Spanish as much as possible. When it comes to programming, read about how to do it, but then put the book down and just do it. If you make a mistake, then refer back to the book for an explanation. Then put the book down and resume with the creation of your program.

The only way to truly learn and to accelerate your learning process is to just do it. Why? Because, as you already know, doing it involves more than just one of our senses while just reading about it only involves one: visual comprehension. This is the difference between mere theoretical knowledge and real-life knowledge. Which knowledge would you prefer?

Your Quick Start Action Step:

What are you so eager to learn, but have been putting off again and again for so long? Reclaim it! Decide right now that you are going to do it without any further delay.

What is something small and concrete that you can shoot for right now? Sit down and plan how long it will take to achieve this goal and start doing it today. All it will take is 30 minutes a day! Schedule that into your calendar right now.

According to your plan, what is the date that you will be able to achieve this goal? How will you feel when you finally succeed at doing it? Write all this down right now to refer back to.

Chapter 2: Setting Up a Better Learning Environment

Chapter 2: Setting Up a Better Learning Environment

2.1

Focus is key to the accelerated learning process, so it is vital that all distractions are removed from the location that you will choose for your learning space. Choosing just one location inside your home or office will cue your brain to get into learning mode whenever you enter this space.

Inside your learning space, you will have all the materials that you need to learn all that you have decided to learn. If you are going to learn how to play the guitar, have your guitar ready-to-go inside your learning space. If you will be working on math, make handy the specific math textbook that you will be using inside your learning space. If you ever have to remove any of these materials from your learning space, always return them back to their place as soon as you can so they are always handy.

Making it as easy as possible for yourself to study and practice will better facilitate the accelerated learning process. The human mind will attempt to find every excuse to not focus, so it's so very important to encourage such focus and attention that is required in every way that you can.

Make sure that your learning space is well lit. Natural light is best, but if you study and learn at night, it's best not to use fluorescent bulbs if you can avoid them. Make sure the light is evenly dispersed and that there is not any glare for your eyes. Open the windows if you can to get the air flowing and oxygen into your brain.

Plants are very soothing to the human mind. Have at least a few in your learning space. They will be yet another source of oxygen for your brain. The sight of any part of nature has a calming effect on our mind. Calm is what you are after when it comes to your learning space.

If you can't get plants to live under your care, artificial ones will do the trick, even if they don't emit the oxygen that real ones do. Anything that reminds you of nature will have a calming effect on you. You can find inexpensive ones at many second-hand stores.

You want your learning space to be neat, tidy and orderly. Physical chaos in this space will distract you and directly affect your learning process, so please attend to this first and foremost.

Make sure you have all the supplies that you need handy so that you do not have to get up and get them from anywhere else or suffer without them. Every interruption will slow down the learning process, so it's so important to make everything as easy for the learning process as possible.

2.2

You will want to inform the people around you about your learning space. It would be best if you have a door to shut the world away. Let everyone around you know that when you close that door, it means that you are working on something very important. Only in an emergency should they ever knock on that door. It's helpful to assure your family, friends, employees, associates or coworkers – whoever the people around you are – that you will be regularly taking breaks and that this will be the ideal time for them to approach you about other less pressing matters.

When you're ready to learn, your learning space always needs to be available to you. If it is not always going to be, then you need to establish at least one alternative learning space. If your learning space changes depending upon conditions, you need to have whatever you need all ready to go along with a bag containing all the smaller required supplies to take with you to your learning space, wherever it is.

Make sure your learning space is a comfortable temperature. There is nothing more distracting to the learning process than being too hot or too cold.

Classical music is a wonderful brain stimulant. You want to be able to bring such music into your learning space. For many, listening to soft Baroque music is very conducive to the thinking process. There are others who swear by Disney piano music. As long as it doesn't have lyrics and isn't distracting, it can work. Experiment with what works for you. The more complex the music, the better it seems to be for our brain.

Make sure your computer is at a good level for typing and that your chair is comfortable to sit in for at least 50 minutes.

Research has shown that humans maintain a better attention span when we break up our work time into 50-minute segments. Thus, a timer is absolutely essential for focus. Whenever the timer goes off, that's when you will know to stop for a 10-minute break, unless, for the moment, you are done with what you are doing. If you struggle with focusing for 50 minutes, try 25 minutes, instead. Everyone is different, so just experiment with what works for you.

Make sure you are doing something completely different during your break time than what you've been working so hard on. For example, if you are writing a book, this would be considered a mental task, so during your 10-minute break, you will ideally want to do something that's not at all mental.

Doing something physical like body stretches, exercising, drinking or eating or something emotional like listening to music or watching a fun, a short video would be a nice change of pace. This is the way that you can allow the area of the brain that you have been utilizing to fully rest while you change gears to use a different part of your brain.

Your Quick Start Action Step:

Evaluate the situation with your learning. Where is your learning space? Do you even have a learning space of your own? Even if you do not have a place where you can shut the door, you can create a space somewhere in your life that when you enter it, your brain knows it's time to learn. Even if it's just turning your nightstand around to make it your desk and carrying everything you need in a bag, begin to plan your learning space right now. If you already have a learning space, how can you improve it to supercharge your learning?

Chapter 3: How to Make Learning Second Nature to You

Chapter 3: How to Make Learning Second Nature to You

3.1

> *"95% of everything you do is the result of habit." – Aristotle*

When was the last time that you drove home and suddenly realized that you didn't remember passing a particular landmark on the way there? This happens to us all the time when something has become a habit. We have driven home so many times that our brain can conserve its resources and go on automatic. Thus, the key to making learning second nature is making it a habit – a way of life.

To learn is to be human... it doesn't matter how old or young you are. The human was built to learn. The truth is, if you were to stop learning, you would die. So, consciously commit right now to being a lifelong learner. When learning truly becomes a habit, we sometimes don't even know that we're doing it. There is no end to what a person can learn, either. No matter what your skill level or IQ, you can learn as much or as little as you want to. There is no limit. Accelerated learning techniques can be used by anyone to better facilitate their particular learning process. If you are human and want to learn more and learn it faster, you definitely will if you put into action even just some of the advice in this book.

One of the best things that you can do for yourself and your brain is to regularly exercise. Research shows that when we are physically active, our brains are able to remember more. Exercise also elevates our mood. And never is it too late to start! All it takes is just a little bit but do as much as you can. Almost anyone can go for a walk every day. Aerobic activity is the best when it comes to our highest brain functions. Commit to doing some kind of aerobic activity for 30 minutes every day. Any person who is truly committed to taking their brain to the next level is going to do this for themselves without fail.

Even more important to your brain than exercise is meditation. So very powerful is the meditation to our brain that it can literally cause our brain to physically grow! So, get meditating, today. Every day, you should spend as much time meditating as you do in exercising. Together, both activities have the potential to totally transform your brain, so greatly accelerating your learning process.

Meditation has been proven to help our brains learn, remember, focus, concentrate, regulate emotion, take on new perspectives, adapt to changing situations, prioritize and make us feel good. In other words, a regular meditation practice improves all aspects of our brain. Combined with the increased blood flow that develops from a regular exercise routine, your brain will just not be able to avoid its highest potential!

3.2 Set up a daily routine for yourself and never deviate from it. Put the mundane on autopilot so that you can focus all your energy on what really matters to you and accelerate your learning process in all your endeavors. To get some ideas, let's find out what the daily routines are of some rather well-known, very smart superachievers:

- Richard Branson:

Wakes up really early every day – when the sun shines through his open curtains at 5:45 am, plays tennis with someone better than him, plays hard and then swims around his island, flies a kite by the ocean, has a healthy breakfast and then is ready for the day.

- Mark Cuban:

Gets up, focuses on his kids, goes to his laptop, reads online and catches up with email, no in- 5-person meetings – everything is done virtually, works out, eats, focuses on his kids and goes to a game

- Elon Musk:

Gets at 7 am, goes to bed at 1 am, starts the day not always with a good breakfast because he doesn't always have time for that, usually has coffee and an omelet that's made for him – no sweet stuff.

- Jack Dorsey (co-founder of Twitter):

Gets up at 5:30 am, meditates and jogs for 6 miles.

- Ariana Huffington:

Meditates for 30 minutes every morning.

- Ellen DeGeneres:

Works out and then meditates for 20 minutes every morning. She says that the quiet and personal time is what gives her the energy to carry out her busy entertainment schedule.

- Mick Jagger:

Works out 6 days per week to reduce stress and keep his stamina up.

- Lady Gaga:

Wakes up, does yoga and 5 minutes of self-directed love and gratitude through compassionate thoughts. She carries the feeling with her throughout the day to stand tall and strong.

- Oprah Winfrey:

Clears her mind with at least 20 minutes of meditation. This gives her more joy and the comfort that there is always the constancy of stillness to return back to amidst all the craziness of the world. This is how she creates her best work and life.

- Will Arnett (actor):

Writes down a gratuity list of 10 things he's thankful for and it always starts with his kids.

- Olivia Wilde (actress):

Begins and ends every day by taking a moment to be grateful.

- Arnold Schwarzenegger:

Starts his day at 5 am, does his workout, eats a healthy breakfast and reads.

- Deepak Chopra (spiritual guru):

Wakes up at 4 am, mediates for 2 hours.

- Stephen King (bestselling author):

Drinks a glass of water or a cup of tea, sits down 8 am – 8:30 am every morning, has his vitamins, listens to music, sits in the same seat with all his papers in the very same place. This helps him to clear his mind and be more focused.

3.3

Here are some more rather well-known, very smart superachiever morning routines:

- Bill Gates:

Doesn't watch much TV, but enjoys reading. While everyone else is watching reality TV, he's busy reading about energy. Starts out his day by spending an hour on the treadmill every day while watching The Teaching Company.

- Mark Zuckerberg (CEO of Facebook):

Enjoys running – spotted in many countries doing this. Always wears the same shirt every morning to avoid decision fatigue.

- Tai Lopez (thought leader):

Thinks your daily routine should be customized according to your situation. What he thinks is universal – 1 part reading (catching up, priming the brain and using your logic) and 2 parts the hardest and most important things you need to do for yourself. He does this first and doesn't put it off. His maximum willpower is in the morning. Doing too difficult things too early in the morning might mean you won't do them that well. He wakes up, catches up with the email from his different companies, goes into reading and acquiring knowledge while eating breakfast and then, a little later, tackles his most important thing.

- Dwayne "The Rock" Johnson:

He does 1 hour of cardio every morning at 4 am.

- Howard Schultz (CEO of Starbucks):

Gets up at 4:30 am and walks his 3 dogs and works out. Says you should use part intuition and part rigor each morning.

Do what is logical for you. Trust some level of your instinct.

- Warren Buffett:

Reads 5-6 hours per day! 5 daily newspapers, some magazines, 5Ks and annual reports. He loves reading biographies.

- Jack Ma (entrepreneur):

Practices Tai Chi – his philosophy for business and life.

- Tony Robbins:

Puts himself "in state" and commands his subconscious mind to help people change their lives NOW. Always is determined to help as many people as possible better their lives. Determines to be the most certain person in the room. Has always imagined the abundance in his life and is so grateful for it. Says that successful people will do what nobody else will. He wakes up, jumps into a hot and cold pool. Primes, meditates, practices gratitude and visualizes the day that he wants.

- Benjamin Franklin:

Woke up at 4 am every day and asked himself what good should he do this day.

- Barack Obama:

Starts his routine 2 hours before events, works out 45 minutes, eats a healthy breakfast, avoids coffee and instead drinks water, orange juice or green tea and avoids all public criticism.

- Steve Jobs:

Looked in the mirror and asked himself if this was the last day of his life, would he want to do what he was going to do that day – if the answer was no, he made immediate changes. Nothing makes accelerated learning a way of life more than a morning ritual. It's the only way to create your best day and best life.

Some key ingredients to an accelerated learner's morning ritual:

1. Set your learning goal for the day.

2. Be committed to getting results and completing all of the steps that will get you there.

3. Always think about the people around you and what they need; always be committed to learning how to fill that need.

4. Do whatever it takes to keep your body and mind at their healthiest and functioning to their full potential.

5. Always tell the truth so you don't always have to waste valuable brain resources covering up your lies and can instead fully focus on the learning task at hand.

6. Do it whether you feel like it or not.

Your Quick Start Action Step:

It's time to come up with your own morning ritual. This is the key to making the accelerated learning process your way of life. Think about all that is most important to you right now. You must start off each day doing this to make sure that it gets done. Body and mind work together as one, so include some sort of physical activity in your morning routine to ensure you get to it every single day. Your accelerated learning process depends upon it! This routine is not etched in stone... as your priorities change, your morning routine will naturally change to follow suit. The most important thing is to start now.

Chapter 4: How to Dramatically Improve Your Study Habits

Chapter 4: How to Dramatically Improve your Study Habits

4.1

A good way to start with your study process is to have a 50 / 25 minute on and 10 minutes off rule. Give your undivided attention to what you are studying for 50 minutes straight and then take a 10-minute break to do something completely unrelated, such as stretching or watching a short funny video. If you cannot hold your focus for that many minutes, try just 25 minutes, instead. Everyone's brain is unique, so you have to do what works for you. But absolutely no multitasking! Some people don't even believe that there is such a thing as multitasking. Never do you ever do anything your best when you're multitasking it. If you're serious about accelerating your learning process, you will save your multitasking for the mundane things that aren't that important to you – if that!

When you sit down to begin studying, you need to have a plan. What are you going to achieve? How are you going to do this? Why are you doing this in the first place? Answering all these questions will help motivate you through the process. If you have already taken the time to create a learning space for yourself, you have already created the environment fit for study. You also will have all the materials that you need to get the job done, saving you so much time. If you are a student, review your syllabus. Make sure that you are going to be studying what is required for your class.

Take out your notes and decide how much of them you are going to go through. Then take out a scrap piece of paper to write down key points that you need to remember as you go through your notes. Read your notes aloud (or in a whisper) and write down all of the key points and ideas on your scrap piece of paper. You are merely writing and rewriting all key points to imprint it upon your brain. It doesn't have to be written neatly. You just have to write all of the information, again and again, to get it inside your brain. As much of your brain that you can activate while doing this, the better. This is how you will remember the information and not forget it. It's also helpful if you have a recording of your class lecture to listen to while you're going through your notes. That's an additional layer of information for another part of your brain to absorb, and this will help you to remember more.

If your notes are from a video that you watched or an audio that you listened to, watch or listen to it again as you go through your notes. It may seem repetitious to go over everything again, but it is such repetition that will hammer the information into your brain. There is no other way to get information to stick inside your brain. This is what all straight A / 4.0 students must do without exception.

4.2

Writing out your own study guide is another good way to retain the information that you study. Again, the act of literally rewriting something helps you to remember it and understand it. Design these study guides in the way that helps you remember all of the information that you're learning. It can be a totally different presentation than what you will find in the book or in class – and this is what you want because you are designing it for your own brain, not anyone else's. Rewriting everything to create your own study guide is the most perfect way to prepare for any test.

It may seem so very tedious to write out everything by hand again and again, but there is no better way to learn. Typing your notes on a laptop will just not do it the same way for you. But if you are in doubt about this, test it out for yourself. If you are like most students, you will find that you will get the best grades in the classes that you manually write notes for again and again. Doing it by hand involves more of your brain and senses which is the goal, especially when it comes to accelerated learning. Really have fun with your study guide and make it beautiful. Just like with your notes, use different colored pens, stickers, and rulers for straight lines. Write the titles in your most beautiful calligraphy. Use all of your creativity because doing so will just be another way for your brain to absorb the information.

Different colors and beauty in your study guide and notes will bring out the joy of learning for you and give you pleasure as well. The more you can associate learning with such joy and pleasure, the more you will accelerate your learning process. Listening to classical music can also be so very conducive to study. If you don't like classical music, any instrumental music that doesn't contain lyrics will do, but the subtle complexities of classical music seem to charge a person's complexity of thought. In terms of accelerated learning, this is exactly what we are after. When you are done with your study session, you need to review how it went. Did you accomplish what you set out to? Are all your questions answered? If not, what additional questions do you have? How will you follow up to get these questions answered? What will you study next time? How much more do you have to study until you feel confident with the material? Make sure to write all the answers to these questions inside a study journal to stay on top of your progress and thoroughly plan your study process.

4.3

The rule is for every hour spent in class, you should spend 2-3 hours studying. The best students always spend the most hours studying, so if you want to accelerate your learning, expect to spend at least 3 hours studying for each and every hour that you spend in class. This number of hours is supposed to include all homework. With that in mind, you might need to spend even more time in a pure study of a subject, especially in preparation for exams. Yes, it's extremely hard work being a straight A / 4.0 student, but there is simply no other way. In the end, you will know the material better than anyone else, and this will eventually direct your career and life. This is expertise, and nothing feels better.

Study takes all your focus so you will want to put away your phone and all distractions. After you have achieved your daily target of study, then you can check your phone and catch up with the people around you. You are not missing anything… you are creating a life that no one else can ever take away from you. This is a skill that you will use for the rest of your life. All the greatest geniuses are always studying. Study becomes a form of play when you do it right. Who needs to go out to the playground to play when your own mind is your playground?

Instead of being depressed and bored like so many of the people around you, you have discovered an exhilarating way of living your life. Who has time to be depressed when there's no end to all you can know about the world around you? You have to see studying as your full-time job. That is what it is.

You are a professional student. No student is better than you are. No one can get in the way of you and your study. Study is a part of who you are. It is your way of life. In order to achieve your highest potential, you have to fully identify with the act of studying. Studying is your way of life. And studying is your greatest joy! It is not an obligation. It is not a chore. It is nothing less than an honor to be given the opportunity to study everything that you choose to. You are in control when you study. No one else is in charge. How many situations in life do you find yourself in total control of? It is a thrill to discover and master new things again and again. And you do it all by yourself without anyone else's direct intervention. The achievement is all yours... and nobody else can ever take that away from you! This is how an accelerated learner views the world and her life. There is nothing that she cannot know or understand. Some subjects require more time to master, but those are the very subjects that are the most rewarding of all.

Your Quick Start Action Step:

It is time for you to set aside a time to study something every day.

Even if you are not a student enrolled in any class, you are a student of life. Commit to learning something specific and plan the steps you need to take to achieve the goal that you set for yourself. What time are you going to set aside every day to study this one thing? Put a half-an-hour study block on your calendar right now, starting today!

Chapter 5: How to Boost your Focus to Laser Precision Levels

Chapter 5: How to Boost your Focus to Laser Precision Levels

5.1

There is no focus when we have more than one task in mind at the same time. You have to practice leaving the world behind, again and again, to achieve laser precision levels of focus on only one task at a time. When you've reached such a level of focus, it's like you are inside your own cocoon. You are in development and cannot come out until what you've focused on is fully resolved – or is, to some degree, at least close to full resolution. Meditation is a practice of focus. There as many ways to meditate as there are things to focus on. The most basic form of meditation focuses on your breath. It seems so very simple, but it can be so challenging for many people. Whenever your mind drifts away to other thoughts, that's when you gently bring it back to your breath. The brain needs some sort of daily practice. Just as one should exercise their body every day, one should exercise their brain every day.

Many people listen to subliminal audios containing affirmations and hypnotic suggestions to rewire their brain. One could even add chanting to their breathing meditation which is a little more advanced. Whatever way you choose to train your brain (and your spirit in the process) will assist you in fine-tuning your mental focus. We aren't taught such techniques in school. As children, we're all commanded to pay attention in the classroom, to concentrate on our homework, but we aren't ever taught how to do just that. We're just left to figure it all out by ourselves. Spiritual practices work so very well with the brain. Whenever you do what it takes to achieve the peace and tranquility that is the natural effect of such practices, you discover peace and tranquility's most pleasant side effect: true focus. What this means is that most of us discover true focus by accident. But let's not live our lives by accident. Without some sort of spiritual, meditative practice, we will never know this true focus. Why do we meditate or have a spiritual practice? To find fulfillment, to become enlightened, to become truly happy... to feel good, naturally. Thus, the laser precision-like focus that you are seeking is the by-product of true happiness.

How do we become truly happy? By looking at ourselves as we are and truly loving what we see. Embracing ourselves just as we are at the core of true happiness. And how does a person do this? By having a spiritual practice that fully illuminates the truth within him. The truth is never outside of yourself. Always is the entire truth within you. Only by way of meditation and/or 8 a spiritual practice can you discover that for yourself. Our energy gets scattered when we look for all our answers everywhere but within ourselves. It is an accelerated learner who would be most prone to doing this. Meditation and spiritual practices put that focus back on ourselves where it always belonged. The whole point of learning is to better ourselves. And why better ourselves? So, we can be of better service to the world around us. We do not have the energy or focus to do such a thing when our own energy is not focused. There is great power in such focus. Even if you don't consider yourself to be at all spiritual, you can instead view the practice of meditation as a mere brain exercise. The extra oxygen that is fed to your brain by all that deep breathing will certainly play a role in your focus.

5.2

Keeping a schedule and staying in control of your time is essential to true focus. No human being can be everything for everyone all the time. We have to be able to figure out the boundaries of our priorities and take each of our priority items one step at a time. If we do not focus on one task and take it step-by-step, we will never get anything done. Of course, we have more than one goal and more than one thing to do. But we have to start somewhere and finish that before moving on to the next thing. We don't want to dabble here and dabble there.

Exploration is fine and necessary, but if you decide something is important enough to actually follow through on and do, finish it! Even if you start something that didn't turn out the way that you thought it would, at least follow through on what you started. Even if it drags on and on without any seeming resolution, you will get more from finishing what you started than you ever would from abandoning it. When you live this way, you are focused. You care about what you start, even if you choose to never start another project of its kind ever again. Finish what you start! Of course, you should not hesitate to quit any job that is totally wrong for you, but at least finishes whatever projects that you started on the job. Even if it takes months, when you finally tie up all of your loose ends, you will walk away from that job feeling like a professional and others won't be able to deny that you are the professional that you are. If we have a healthy mind and spirit, we are going to have so many interests. But when it comes to starting your first business, it's important to start with one career or niche.

You may be a multi-talented genius, but if you don't pick just one of your many specialties to focus on when you professionally launch yourself, your business will lack the focus that you need to make money. You can't be all things you want to be, especially when you're just starting out. You have to pick one thing. It's kind of like you cannot be in more than one place at a time. As you get known for one thing, then you can branch out to add other layers to your career and niche, later. So many entrepreneurs do this, but only after they have become known and have earned a decent amount of money in one specialty niche. That is the way business works. This is also the way that the human mind works. We have to associate a business with one niche so that we will know where to file it inside our brain. But Amazon will buy Whole Foods, and ATT will acquire CNN. So, in truth, there is no business that works in only one niche. It's our minds that can't resist labeling everything with just one color or another. If our minds try to mix all the many colors together, we end up with some weird hue of brown or black.

5.3

As a student, you will eventually have to choose what field you want to focus on if you haven't already. You have to choose one major and stick with it or be forced to take more classes and stay in college longer. The most talented students struggle with this choice. Most college students are only 18-years-old when they enter college... how is an 18-year-old supposed to know what to do with the rest of their life? You don't! Just choose one place to start. And once you start somewhere, follow through with your choice. If you don't, the lack of focus and the lack of commitment that comes with it will weigh you down for years to come. What if you find out that a major is not at all what you expected. Well, if you really gave it a go, then you have a lot more information about this subject matter than you did when you began. Follow your intuition and do what feels right.

There is nothing wrong with changing your major. Just follow through on your commitments in your old major before changing direction to go into a new major. A focus has intention, purpose, and finality. It is committed to whatever it does, even if it completely changes its direction and course. What do you want to learn? Why do you want to learn it? How will it help to further your goals? How does it fit in with everything else that you have already spent so much time to learn? Does this subject excite you? Why? If it excites you so much, why haven't you studied it before?

Answering these questions and more can give your life and studies so much more focus and direction. Go to the dollar store and purchase a journal to write in... or spend more if you prefer. The practice of journaling can be so very enlightening. Laser precision focus does not only apply to the way that we should study, it also applies to the way we should make our decisions and live our lives.

Your Quick Start Action Step:

Go to the dollar store and get that journal I spoke about. Start journaling about the life you want to live. What are you doing? What are your priorities? How are you going to focus yourself enough to get what you want? How are you going to structure your day to produce the results that you dream of? What are the other things that you love, but won't be pursuing? Why? Only you have the answers to all these questions... so write, read and study them!

Chapter 6: Easy Techniques to Remember Facts and Figures – Fast

Chapter 6: Easy Techniques to Remember Facts and Figures – Fast

6.1

We, humans, are visual creatures, so the way to remember anything is to create a visual image for it. Such an association created to aid in the memory process is known as a mnemonic. The way to remember facts and figures fast is to first take the time to attach an image to the numbers 1-20 and each and every letter of the alphabet. You need to be so familiar with these associations that you know them backward and forwards, so the preparation for this will take some time. After you have done this, you then need to create a map for yourself. A good place to start is your house. You will need more than one room, but some of us only live in a one-room apartment... so know that you can create this map from anywhere. Collect places in your mind until you have about 5 spaces that have at least 5 objects inside them. Let's say the first space we're talking about your living room. Pick 5 objects inside your living room to use for your map: the lamp by the door, the sofa, the rug, the picture over the sofa and the piano. Do this for 5 rooms or spaces.

Picture in your mind which objects you will use in each room or space. Then, when you need to instantly memorize facts or figures, just attach them to the appropriate image that you have created. For instance, let's say you need to remember a long serial number. Bring up the image you have created for each digit of that serial number, one at a time, and associate them with each of the different objects in each room or space that you have prepared for your map. This gives each number or letter in the serial number an image as well as a location on your map. This is known as a mind palace, first made popular by Sherlock Holmes. A mind palace works perfectly with the way that our brain is wired. If you need to remember someone's name, focus on the first letter of this name and use the image that you have created for this letter. For example, if the name you need to remember is Beatrice, associate Beatrice with the image you have created for the letter B.

Then associate that with the first object in your first room or space. If you're concerned that the letter B won't remind you of the full name, you could spell out the name with each of the images you have created for every letter in her name and then associate each of those letters in the 1st, 2nd, 3rd, 4th and 5th objects in your first room or space and continue spelling it and associating the images you created with the 1st, 2nd and 3rd objects in your second room or space until the name is fully spelled. Or you could just simply associate her name with an image of a bee to help you remember her full name and then attach that bee to the first object in your first room or space in your mind palace. It sounds very tedious and not very fast at all, but once you have become so familiar with all the images that you have created for 1-20 and each letter of the alphabet, it's very automatic. It just requires quite a bit of prep time. You can also simply pick one of the images that you have already created to associate with a name or any other piece of information as a memory aid. Like an X marks the spot for the name, Mark, for example.

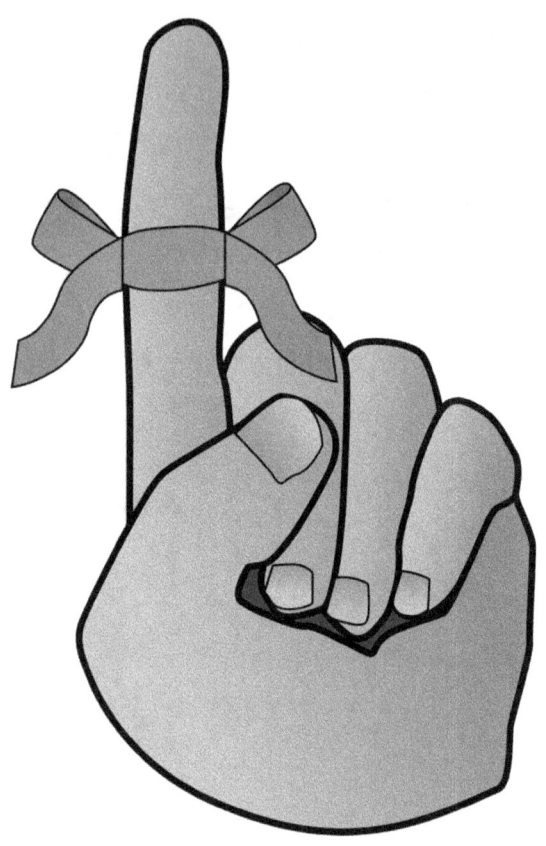

6.2

When you write something over and over again, you engrave it upon your brain. It might not be as fast as the previous method once you have a set of images in mind to draw from, but for those of us who have more trouble seeing images inside their mind, writing something again and again on a piece of paper also helps you to remember. Any way that you can turn numbers or words into pictures really helps your brain out. This is why it's so helpful to use lots of colors in the notes that you take. The color and pictures actually help you to remember.

When we don't use information more than once, it's automatically put in our short-term memory, and this is why we forget it so easily. If we really want to remember something, we need to use it more than once so that our brain puts it in our long-term memory. Thus, as soon as we learn something that we don't want to forget, we should immediately repeat it – go over it again – even though it feels like we already remember it. Then, we should go over it again in 15-20 minutes and again 6-8 hours later. Finally, go over it one last time in 24 hours. Again, this is not as fast as the first method, but it does work. Now, if you want to remember something for a long time, it's slightly different.

Once you learn it, you want to go over it again right after learning it, then again in 20-30 minutes. Then wait for a day before going over it again and then go over it again in 2-3 weeks. In 2-3 months, go over it one last time. Understand what you learn and make sure you are learning what's most important. Something to keep in mind when studying is that you will remember the beginning and the end best.

Switching activities every 15-20 minutes will also help you remember what you are learning. In language, learning opposite things is helpful because you can memorize them in pairs.

Memorizing associated words in a language like a tie, suit, shoes, and briefcase can assist in the memory process as well. You can also make up stories by connecting all the pieces of what you are learning together in some sort of plot. Another idea is to record yourself reading all your notes. If you listen to the recording a few times, you will be activating more parts of your brain to remember than if you just read your notes silently. Visualizing the information is always memorable to the mind, but make sure you use only the latest information before you memorize anything.

6.3

Another memory technique is to assign bizarre images to parts of your body in sequential order. Let's say you're a teacher who wants to remember all of the students according to seat in your classroom. What you can do is come up with a visual that helps you to remember each of their names according to the order that they sit in. Johnny who sits in the last seat could be assigned to your feet who repeat, "Here's Johnny!" as in Johnny Carson. Christine who sits next to him could be assigned to your knees and take the form of the cross to make you think of Christ... or Christine.

This is how your body can be used as a mind palace. You can also read information again and again and then write it out in your own words and read it out loud again and again. Draw pictures and diagrams to help you remember it and then think up a mnemonic phrase or acronym that helps you remember the information. Take an hour break and then return back to the material.

There is also the major system method that connects numbers with letters that you connect to images. It seems so cumbersome, but memory champions actually use this method to memorize long string of numbers. Each number is assigned a letter, and you take the numbers in chunks of 3 and convert them into their assigned letters. These letters don't usually spell anything, but they always remind you of a word which you then use to assign an image to each chunk of 3 numbers. Rather than use your own home or your body, if you're serious about memorization, you can use a dollhouse to build your mind palace.

Place your assigned images in sequential order throughout, starting on the front porch and going in order around each and every room. For this to work, you do have to take the time to remember what numbers are assigned to what letters whose spelling remind you of the assigned images. Another technique is to walk around your city or town and create a mind palace along your journey from point A to point B. You could create an endless number of mind palaces in this way. Mind palaces are everywhere!

Your Quick Start Action Step:

Pick your favorite memory hack described in this chapter and test it out by memorizing a long list of your choice. How did that particular technique work for you? Now, try a different technique to see if it works 6 better for you. This can be a lot of fun, and you might even end up amazing yourself. Perhaps this is the way that you will now tackle all memorization going forward. Everyone is different… find the way that works best for you!

Chapter 7: Strategies for Better Listening

Chapter 7: Strategies for Better Listening

7.1

Listening well requires that you are actively involved in what you are hearing. You are motivated by what you are hearing, you are making sense of what you are hearing, and you are not allowing yourself to be distracted.

In The Seven Habits of Highly Effective People by Stephen Covey, he says: "... you must listen with your eyes and with your heart. You must listen for feeling as well as for meaning. You must listen for behavior. You must use your right brain as well as your left. You sense you intuit, you feel..." When you listen, you are not simply hearing the words that are being said. There is a whole other layer of communication that comes with the words that you are hearing and it is important to understand this.

True listening doesn't only involve your rational mind, it involves your whole brain. When you are truly listening to someone, you are observing and interpreting their body language, the tone of voice, the expression upon their face and their hand movements. Sometimes we misunderstand the intended message, so it's very important to ask questions. If you're in a class, such questions can inform the instructor that you are actively listening to their presentation. It is your responsibility as an accelerated learner to make sure that you have properly understood what your teacher has communicated.

To listen well is not to be passive. It takes a lot of effort to clearly understand what someone is saying. Some of the problems we have are that our brain has a faster process time than what a person can speak.

Our brains can process 400- 500 words per minute, but a person can only speak about 100-250 minutes per minute. As the listener, this causes our minds to wander and get distracted. Instead, we should use this time to fully observe all the other layers of human communication that come with speech, but we usually don't. And this is why we only remember about 25% of what we hear. There are different levels of attention that we bring to listening:

Listening unconsciously means that we don't even hear what is being said. We are totally focused on other things.

Listening superficially means that we hear the sound of the person speaking to us, but don't understand what is being said and are distracted by other things. Listening while evaluating means that we are trying to understand what is being said, but we are merely concerned with the content while ignoring all other information in the message. Listening actively means that we are focused on the true intention of the speaker's words and message. We are not attempting to judge the speaker or his message, we are attentively processing the speaker's intended message in all its entirety.

7.2

Focus is such a vital part of active listening. Whenever you feel the urge to interrupt what is being said, first breathe deeply. Besides preventing you from speaking to interrupt, this will get more oxygen into your brain to help you focus further. Decide that you are going to pay attention and participate in the conversation. You can mirror the speaker by rephrasing what he is saying when it's your time to speak. This confirms your understanding of what was said and lets the speaker know that you are listening to him. Look into the speaker's eyes as he communicates with you. This is the way that you show your interest in what he is saying.

Combine this with your nonverbal reactions to all he is saying… smile, laugh, nod, raise your eyebrows and lean forward to fully communicate your interest in what he is saying. Encourage the speaker to continue communicating with you and ask him questions to clear up any misunderstandings. Freely offer your feedback to what he is saying and enlarge the scope of the conversation as appropriate.

Be interested in knowing more. Even though it is he who speaks, this is an exchange of ideas between him and you. Without you, there would be no communication. Focus on what you agree on and have in common, first and foremost. If what he says upsets you, visualize yourself being the picture of calm. In true communication, everyone wants and needs to be at ease. It's really amazing, but research shows that 90% of the speaker's message will not be contained in his words. To get active with our listening, we can compare different aspects of what the speaker is telling us. What are the advantages or disadvantages of what he is saying? What is positive, what is negative? What is your opinion in comparison to what the speaker is expressing?

We can also listen to the sequence of events, facts or ideas that the speaker conveys and the way that he orders and prioritizes them. We can make note of all the important points that the speaker is communicating to us and how he is backing these up. Make sure that you understand all the words that the speaker uses as well as their connotations. Never hesitate to ask questions when you're not sure about something. If anything, such questions will only inform the speaker that you care enough about what he is saying to do the work necessary to truly understand his message.

The act of good listening has become similar to a lost art. When we truly listen, we literally create meaning out of sound. Pattern plays a very important role in this. It's how we distinguish something that we need to listen to from noise. For example, we always look up whenever we hear our name.

Each of us also has our own set of unconscious filters that we use when we listen to the world around us that helps to shape our own reality. Some of these filters might be our culture, the language that we speak, the values that we hold dear, our beliefs, our attitude, our expectations, and intentions – bad or good. It's really interesting, too, that sound always places us in a particular time and space. Always is there a thread of the time weaved into all the sound that we hear. In fact, the sound is one of the primary ways that we experience time.

"Sonority is time and meaning." – Jean-Luc Nancy

A lot of the reason why we are losing the art of listening is that, nowadays, we can make audio or video recordings of anything that we wish to. In ancient times, people didn't have this convenience, of course, but were somehow able to remember vast amounts of information that were verbally conveyed to them well enough to write down. Before there were any writing systems, all teachings were expounded by way of sound, and somehow large enough groups of people were able to remember enough of what they heard to be able to pass it down to us, today. It's really quite remarkable. Can you imagine if you had to get all your information from live presentations that you only had the opportunity to watch once?!

Today, our world is so noisy thanks to our digital madness. We demand sound bites because we no longer have the patience to truly listen to someone's full intended message. It's like we are becoming deaf, forcing advertisers to use one word in all caps as headlines to capture our attention. It's like we've totally lost our ability to notice all the soft and subtle shades of our communication. This is a crisis because listening is the original way that humans learned.

Before there were writing systems before there was language... we listened! Without language, it was vitally important that our ancestors listened consciously to pick up on every one of the many cues that they needed to survive. Such conscious listening is the path to understanding and learning for our species. Practice being silent every day. You need to be able to hear the quiet.

Count all the many layers of sound that you hear in a noisy environment. Savor all of the many mundane sounds around you. Julian Treasure calls all of these marvelous sounds, "the hidden choir." An acronym that Julian came up to help leaders, teachers, spouses, parents, and friends (that's just about all of us, right?) remember how to listen is RASA. This is the Sanskrit word for juice or essence: Receive, Appreciate, Summarize, Ask. Schools need to teach students how to listen. It needs to be in the curriculum. Human communication is the only path to the true connection and understanding that will bring about true world peace, one person at a time.

Being able to listen well is a skill you can use in all areas of life. Once you know how to truly listen to a person, you will know how to be her friend, her spouse, her parent, her co-worker, her boss, her teacher, her student, her colleague, her customer or business associate. You cannot have a successful relationship with anyone if you do not know how to listen to them and hear what they intend to communicate.

Accelerate your learning and accelerate all your relationships when you learn how to actively listen.

Your Quick Start Action Step:

Practice your listening skills by going to YouTube and listening to a 15-minute video on something you're interested in. Watch it all the way through and pay attention. Bookmark the page and do something else. The next day, return back to the same video and watch it again. Does the video leave you with the very same meaning this time? If it doesn't – why? What did you do differently this time that changed your understanding and perception of the message?

If your understanding of the video seems to be the same the second time around, play the video once more and pay special attention to the speaker's facial expressions, body language, emphasis and vocal tone. Watch the video like you have never seen it before. See if you come away from it understanding their message any differently. If you heighten your awareness, you will notice subtle pieces of information you never noticed when you watched the video the first couple of times. There are always so many layers to the learning process!

Chapter 8: Write and Retain – Better Note Taking

Chapter 8: Write and Retain – Better Note Taking

8.1

Taking notes is absolutely essential to learning anything. In Chapter 1, we went over how our brain works and why we remember so much more when we involve as many of our senses as possible in the learning process. Note taking does exactly that. You are listening, you are seeing things on the board or in your book or maybe on a video, and you are seeing the notes that you kinesthetically manufacturing with your hands.

Together, all this involves the auditory, visual and kinesthetic parts of your neocortex to cement what you are learning into your brain, making it far more likely that you will actually remember it. Even if you were to never look at your notes ever again, the very act of taking these notes has helped you to internalize the information in these notes.

Sometimes, you don't even have to refer back to your notes to remember them. If you tend to be more visual, you might even be able to see the notes in your mind and remember some of the information that way. Taking notes also helps you to actively engage in whatever you are learning. You are forced to focus enough to recreate on paper what you are hearing and seeing. It is this active focus that involves enough of the brain to activate the accelerated learning process. And the more thorough your notes are, the better. Start by going over everything that you will be learning ahead of time – before ever taking any notes. Familiarize yourself with the material and all its ideas, vocabulary and terms.

Allow your brain to sort through everything to get a sense of what is important and what is less so. This may mean that you will be watching a video once through before watching it again to take notes. Or maybe you will be watching parts of a video before stopping to take notes and rewinding when necessary. It really depends on you and how you learn best. You just make it easier for your brain to organize the information when you first give it an introduction to this information. Humans tend to be visual, so get visual with your notes! Your brain will remember more if you use different colors and pictures to explain the information that you are recording. You can do this as you are taking your notes or add stickers and images when you are reviewing these notes later on. This will make note taking so much more fun, and the information will be more apt to really stick inside your mind. This is so natural for kids to do and this is some of the reason why they learn so very easily. Be like a kid and have some fun!

8.2

When you take notes, make sure you don't merely copy what's written on the board or in your book. Listen for the main ideas and put them in the paper efficiently, so you can easily understand the meaning later. When in a classroom or watching a video with someone teaching with a blackboard, whiteboard or paper on an easel, you will miss a lot of very valuable information if you only write what they do.

Listen carefully to the important points that they stress. You need to write them down, even if they don't write it on their board. You'll want to develop your own shorthand to indicate when something is going to be on a test or is something you need to review later. Have fun with your notes and really make them your own.

Purchasing different colored pens and pencils can help you color code different entries. Stickers and your little doodles can really bring your notes to life, especially when you're reviewing them later. Highlighter pens are also great. Sticky notes are also helpful and try different notebooks and different ways of putting your notes upon the page. These are your notes, and there are no rules. Being creative affects your entire study process, helping the information to sink in more deeply. If learning is going to be your way of life, you might as well enjoy it and have some fun.

When you have fun, you learn so much more without realizing it. As soon as you can, you need to review your notes after taking them. This really solidifies the concepts inside your mind, so you remember them better later. Any places where you left details out, fill in the gaps. If something isn't clear, make it clear. If there is missing information that you can't remember, make note of it so you can look it up or ask someone about it. Once you get your answer, be sure to update your notes so you won't forget it. If you are a student, many students find it very helpful to record their lectures.

To be legal about this, check with your teacher or professor to make sure they're okay with you doing this. If they are, record all your lectures to go back over again later. Some students won't even take notes while in class if they're recording it, waiting until later to do so, but you will better facilitate your learning process if you do take notes while in class and then later fine-tune them while listening to the recording. And, who knows... there could be some kind of malfunction or glitch that prevents the lecture from getting recorded.

You will never go wrong if you always take notes. When your teacher draws a diagram on the board, take a picture of it with your phone instead of attempting to draw it directly into your notebook in the limited time that you have during the lecture. Put all the notes that go with the diagram onto a separate piece of paper so that when you take the time to properly draw the diagram into your notebook later on, everything's far neater and more legible, making study time so much easier for yourself.

8.3

Some students like to completely rewrite their notes because it helps them learn and retain the information better. When they rewrite them, they use non-line paper and take the time to make their notes beautiful and organized. Allow your creativity to flow, and you will find that you will retain so much more information in the process. Use a ruler or protractor to create clean, straight lines and different colored pens using a color code system that works for you.

If you know calligraphy, it's really fun to put it to use to make your notes pop. Writing your notes in list form can make them so much easier to read. Use bullet points, hyphens, and boxes. Sticky notes are also good for definitions. You can cut them to just the right size for the page. It's also helpful to name your diagrams using the chapter number and unit number so that you can refer back to them in your notes whenever you need to. Use your highlighter for subtopics and clean, straight lines to separate all topics.

When dealing with PowerPoint slides, it's always great to get a copy of them to print out so you can add your notes to all the visuals from a presentation or lecture. This can also assist in the memory process since our memory is driven by images. Print them out with two slides to a page to give you the right amount of space for your notes. It may seem like doing all of this will take so much time, but it is time well invested if you are truly serious about accelerating your learning process.

There is no one who can just walk into a class or watch a video and get it all the first time. Our brains just do not work that way. Yes, some of us might have a photographic memory or be able to listen to a lecture or training like a tape recorder, but I guarantee that you will not be able to fully retain the information that you are exposed to unless you take the time to do what it takes to remember everything in the long-term. The student who is a true genius does whatever it takes to take their knowledge to the next level at all times. You will not ever be able to fully exhibit your genius until you work really hard.

No one would ever know that someone was a genius if they never did the work that it takes to reach the genius levels of any subject matter. If a genius doesn't care to do any of the work that it takes, he or she will never be able to achieve anything more than anyone else. Yes, even geniuses have to work hard like this. For all you know, you might be one of them... but you'll never find out if you don't take the time to do all the work that is necessary.

Your Quick Start Action Step:

Go to the dollar store and buy an inexpensive notebook for each of the subjects that you are studying. Then, purchase some markers and pens in the colors that catch your attention.

Buy a ruler or protractor to draw straight lines with and maybe some fun stickers as well. Then, if you feel moved, purchase another unlined notebook for each of your subjects for rewriting your notes in a creatively neat way that properly organizes the information for your unique brain. Then, when you get home, have fun creating a system template for your rewritten notes using all the materials that you just bought!

Chapter 9: How to Achieve Superb Reading Comprehension

Chapter 9: How to Achieve Superb Reading Comprehension

9.1

If you are a student, it's always good to review your syllabus before you begin your reading. By doing so, you get a feel for the plan that your instructor has for their presentation of the course material. How much are you expected to read per week? How is the book broken down into reading segments? Next, go over the book's table of contents and go to the various sections and chapters to get a feel for how the book is structured.

Flip through the chapters and glance at the material. How long are the chapters? Will you be reading them in the order found in the book? What will be included in the assigned homework? Now, find out what your reading assignment is and begin reading. If you can write in your book, use highlighters and underline key points, but also take notes to really absorb the material as much as you can the first time that you read it.

There are a lot of speed readers out there, but PhotoReading is by far the most efficient way to read fast and most fully comprehend what you read. PhotoReading utilizes the power of your subconscious mind which far supersedes the conscious mind that you use when you utilize speed reading techniques.

After you have gotten a good overview of how the course and book are structured as described, above, the next step is to establish your purpose for reading the book. You need to verbalize this purpose to yourself, so your subconscious can hold it in mind as you read the book.

Now, open the book at the beginning and examine the front and back cover, the title page and table of contents. Again, look at the chapters and observe the book's structure. Now it's time to look at the first page like you are taking a picture of it. Then turn to the next page to do the same and keep doing this in a rhythmical fashion with each and every page until you get to the very last page of the book. You should spend about one second on each page. It may not feel like it, but your subconscious mind really did take a picture of each and every page of the book that you turned to.

The images of each and every page that you turned to are now inside your brain. Now, turn the book upside down and turn the book over so that the back cover faces up. Now rhythmically turn to each page for one second like you did start from the beginning of the book when it was upright. Yes, your mind really can read upside down! It's time to turn the book upright again and go over it like you did in the beginning. All you're doing is re-familiarizing yourself with the structure of the book to reactivate your conscious mind and, thus, connect it with your subconscious mind. Look at the front and back cover, the title page and table of contents. Now, take your finger and move it down each page until a word or phrase pops out at you. Write these words down. Move your finger down each page and create a list of all the words and phrases that pop out of the text.

Take this list and write out the questions that they inspire. This will help to guide your process of learning the material. This is the time to walk away from the book to give your brain some time to process. Return back to the book no sooner than in 20 minutes, but it's best to wait until the very next day after you have slept. Again, familiarize yourself with the structure of the book and then activate the book in your mind by super reading with your moving finger down each page. When you come across a word or phrase that pops out at you, do what they call dipping... start reading that section more deeply until that word or phrase is adequately explained. You can put this information in your notes.

Keep doing this throughout the entire book, and you will have a firm grasp of the material. Mind maps work really well with this method, and it's good to use different colors to help your brain process the information. It's rather remarkable that our schools don't teach us how to do this. If more people knew how to read like this, so many more people would read on a regular basis and society would benefit from the expertise of so many.

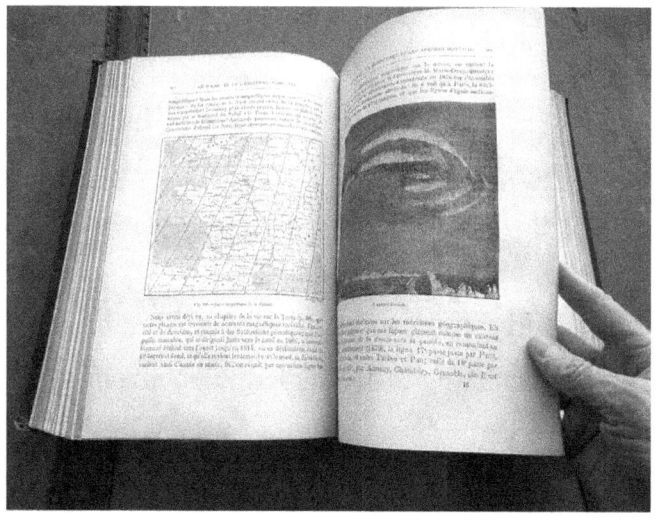

9.2

Think of how many more books you could get around to reading using this photo reading technique. Of course, there will always be those books you prefer to take the time to fully savor, but think of how much more deeply you will absorb such reading treasures when you begin the reading process by applying this PhotoReading technique.

I am just giving you an overview of the technique, but if you are really serious about it, there are courses dedicated to it and groups of people committed to perfecting it. It was Paul Scheele of Learning Strategies in Minneapolis, Minnesota who first developed photoreading over 20 years ago and he has gotten it down to a science.

PhotoReading is quite natural for some people and not so natural for others. If you are intuitive, you already allow your subconscious mind to guide you so photoreading will feel the most natural to you. However, if you tend to solely rely upon your analytical mind for information, you might find it rather difficult to calm your mind down to the point of receiving information from a deeper place inside of you. That's why there are programs out there designed to help you master this most crucial skill which most of us have yet to even discover.

When you know how to photo read, you do not need speed reading techniques. Just like you can "take a picture" of an entire page of words with your mind, you can do the same with a line of words or a paragraph. And because you are leveraging the power of your subconscious mind, your reading comprehension is far greater than it would be if you read the material in any other manner. Did you know that the subconscious mind can process 40 million bits per minute while the conscious mind can only process 40 bits per minute? That is why PhotoReading is the very best way to learn the material you are reading. Your subconscious mind will bring to your attention what is most crucial in the text in relation to the purpose you established before beginning.

9.3

When you get really good at PhotoReading, you can have a very good understanding of an entire book in about an hour or so and can read groups of books simultaneously in a very short period of time. PhotoReading is the solution for all researchers and students. It's really surprising that this innovative reading technique hasn't become more well-known by now. Will you please help spread the word? You are an accelerated learner, so it is your goal to innovate your learning process in every way that you can. This takes time and commitment.

Most people in our society don't have faith in their ability to learn and would have difficulty believing that they could be successful reading in this way. PhotoReading is not just for geniuses. All of us have a subconscious mind and a conscious mind – all that's required for PhotoReading. It's just that our schools teach us to read in only one way and, because of this, we believe that is the only way that we can read. Our study of the subconscious mind is still so very new. We still are stuck in so many old, inefficient ways of doing things that are limited by our conscious minds.

The freedom that PhotoReading gives us is nothing short of revolutionary. Let's hope there comes a time when PhotoReading is the way that children are taught to read, and we all can look back and smile wondering how we ever got by without it. That is the way all technologies and innovations change us.

Your Quick Start Action Step:

1. Take a non-fiction book that is not too long and experiment with photo reading it. Look at the front and back cover, the title page and the table of contents.

2. Familiarize yourself with the way that the book is structured, then,

starting with the first page, turn to each page and "take a picture" of it with your mind. Only spend one second on each page until you get to the very last page.

3. Then, turn the book upside down and turn it over so that the back cover faces up.

4. Now turn to each page like you just did, but, this time, going backward through the upside-down book.

5. Once done, turn the book upright and re-familiarize yourself with the structure of the book from the beginning before moving your finger down each page until a word or phrase pops out at you.

6. Write these words and phrases down and keep going until you get to the end of the book.

7. Now ask yourself what the book is about. Can you write a summary? You will surprise yourself at how well you know the material after only a few minutes of photo reading!

Chapter 10: Boost Your Learning with Mathematics

Chapter 10: Boost your Learning with Mathematics

10.1

To learn math, we have to do it for ourselves. This is the way that life is as well. The only way that we learn to live life is by living life for ourselves. You cannot live your life without failing and be failing again, and math is just like that. Mathematics is such a very safe place to practice failure! Math actually teaches us how to fail and then find the success in that failure.

There is always a solution to every math problem and, likewise, there is always a solution to every problem we encounter in life. If we cannot fail, we cannot find success. Never underestimate the value of failure. Without failure, there is no success! So, math can be the perfect laboratory for the failure we need to master in order to live a better life. Math teaches us how to bounce back and recover. How you recover can become so important to your life as well. If you find math to be boring, you most likely will also find life to be boring. It's not all the time that we find excitement, and this is part of the definition of excitement... it doesn't happen all the time.

Honestly, wouldn't it be boring if everything was always exciting all of the time?! When you get bored, you play to amuse yourself and, when you play in math, you discover all sorts of fun patterns. A play is how humans learn and play is how you will accelerate your learning process.

To solve a difficult math problem, you have to get creative and try to solve it yourself to learn the most from it. If you just wait for your instructor to publish the solutions, you will not learn nearly as much from looking at his solutions. Everyone has their own unique solution to a math problem. The key to learning is finding your own unique solution to all of your problems. Just like in math, in life, we have to take responsibility for ourselves, our actions, our relationships, our learning and our life.

Check this out:

Let's say you are 4 years old and start playing video games for 2 hours-a-day. By the time that you graduate from high school, you will have spent a total of more than 10,000 hours playing video games. Compare this to how much time it would take you to earn your bachelor's degree with a 4.0: 6,000 hours! The math just has a way of putting everything into perspective, doesn't it? In math, you have to use your full brain to solve problems, and it is the very same in life. There is no more humbling experience than math, either. You think you know all that there is to learn and you find out that there's no end to how much more there is to learn. Hey, that sounds a whole lot like life, doesn't it? It's when you discover this that math gets exciting... and it's the same with life.

The complexity of a difficult math problem makes it so very clear that you are not the center of the universe, much like a difficult life experience does. In math, we have to fail before we can succeed, we have to practice it and dedicate ourselves to it and work really hard at it. It humbles us, it forces us to abandon the superficial to discover its depth.

It encourages us to investigate, get creative and play and it's a very personal experience... just like life! So, you see, there are few better ways than math to prepare for a successful life full of learning. If we can find a way to truly enjoy computing all of our future possibilities with math, we will better understand and enjoy the life that we live in and the world that we live in.

10.2

Mathematics is life at its core. All of the world around us has its foundation in math. It is the building blocks of our existence. It is the idea behind life as we know it.

Nature is science and science is mathematics.

Math is everywhere. It's really good at making connections. Math is all the pure ideas behind reality.

Equations create connections. Infinity is found in fractals.

You can never see a fractal in all its entirety, you can only get the sense of it. Fractals can be found all around us in snowflakes and so many biological forms. They are even employed in the art.

Pi – the circle – is the center of so many equations and as well as our universe.

Equations are relationships.

Algebraic equations are at the very core of science and engineering.

A vector is a matrix.

The matrix is all around us. A matrix is a structure.

Your body has matrices within it, including your brain.

Search engines use matrices to produce their results. A matrix can even show all the connections in your brain. Matrices also create structure. This math is omnipresent and everywhere. Math is not all about the numbers. Every day a new idea is created in math.

Math is actually a creative act. Math is more flexible and open-ended than you can ever imagine. It is an art. There are great composers in Math, but no one plays Math, according to Masao Morita. He came up with the idea of holding math concerts in coffee houses so that it's not only the professional mathematicians who can appreciate the true beauty of Math.

Did you know that the number one cannot be proven? The number one is merely an idea that we all believe in. Math is about engaging with your inner universe. Look at a Math problem and solve it yourself without anyone else's help.

Look within yourself for the answer. When you do, that is what Math is all about.

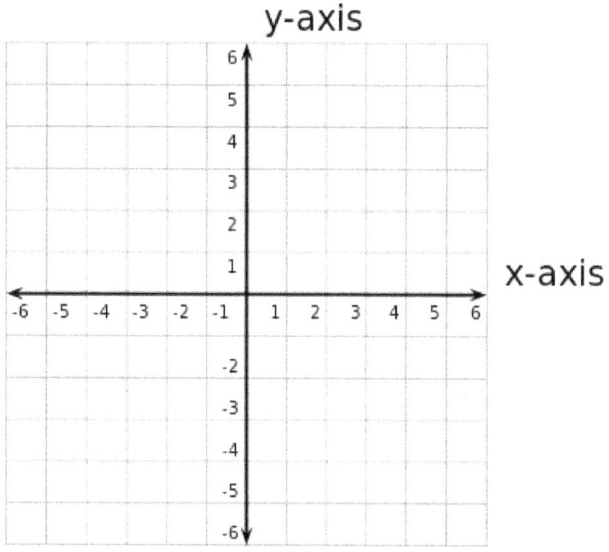

10.3

"Make your calculations before the battle, because who does them well will win. Thorough calculations triumph over inadequate ones." – *Sun Tzu, Chinese sage.*

A really wonderful way to assess new projects is to use the whymap that was originally created by Descartes in 1600. We all learn about the whymap in Math class, but for some reason, we never put it to use in our daily lives.

Make a detailed list of all the bad and good effects that a project will have on you. Be sure to not leave the smallest detail out. Next, make a list of all the bad and good effects this same project will have on others.

Now go back to the list you made about you and rate each effect on a scale from 1 to 100, 100 being the most intense. Add up all the rating numbers of the good effects and subtract from this number the sum total of all the rating numbers of the bad effects.

Next, divide the number you get by the total number of effects, whether good or bad. Draw a graph and place this resulting number on the vertical axis. Now do the same for all the rating numbers for others.

Put this resulting number on a graph on the horizontal axis. For perspective, draw a straight light through zero from the lower left quadrant up to into the upper right quadrant. The more efficient your project is for yourself and others, the higher your point will be in the central upper right quadrant. Likewise, the least efficient your project is for yourself and others, the lower down it will be in the central lower left quadrant.

Any point in the middle of all the quadrants is neutral.

This can be a science in and of itself! Where does your project stand? If it's not where you want it to be, what can you do to tweak the numbers, so it's where you want it to be?

Your Quick Start Action Step:

It's time to evaluate a project that you've been pondering and considering with a why map!

List all the good and bad effects it will have on yourself and all the good and bad effects it will have on others. Now rate each of these effects on a scale of 1 to 100, 100 being the most intense. Add up all the rating numbers for the good effects for you and all the ratings for the bad effects for you and then subtract the resulting number for the bad effects for you from the resulting number for the good effects for you. Then, do the exact, same thing for the good and bad effects for others.

The final number you get for you needs to be divided by the total number of effects, whether good or bad. Once you get this final number, create a graph and plot it on the vertical axis. Now, do the same for the final number you get for others and plot on your graph the horizontal axis. Draw a straight line through zero from the lower left quadrant up into the upper right quadrant for perspective.

Whatever point you get on your graph is the extent that your project is efficient for you and others. The more efficient your project is, the higher your project will be in the central upper right quadrant. Likewise, the least efficient your project is, the lower it will be in the central lower left quadrant. Any point in the middle of all the quadrants is neutral. Where is your project?

Chapter 11: How to Avoid Learning Mistakes

Chapter 11: How to Avoid Learning Mistakes

11.1

> *"Anyone who has never made a mistake has never tried anything new." – Albert Einstein.*

Is a mistake really a mistake? We as humans could never learn anything if we didn't ever make a mistake. The way to avoid mistakes is to see each and every inevitable mistake in the learning process as an opportunity to learn something new. This is the ultimate goal of the accelerated learning process, is it not? Who was it who said, "to err is to be human"? That seems to be a paraphrase of Alexander Pope: "To err is human; to forgive, divine." But it's definitely foolish to make unnecessary mistakes. What are mistakes that we can avoid? Well, when we are learning, there are many things that we are still ignorant of.

Even experts in a field can harbor some ignorance about the subject of their expertise. It is impossible to know everything about anything, so each and every one of us will sometimes have some ignorance. This is the nature of learning something new.

The mistake we can avoid is not giving a subject matter our full attention. If we are going to the trouble to study something or take a class, why wouldn't we go to the trouble to give it the attention it deserves? Are you attempting to multitask? Do you really think that you can do more than one thing well? No one should ever try to multitask when they are studying. You are not studying if you are dividing your attention elsewhere. Multitasking has been over-rated in our society. If we are too busy to put our full attention on whatever we are doing, we are too busy and need to cut back.

You are a human being with a brain who cannot do more than one thing at a time very well. You may consider yourself to be a really great multi-tasker, but I guarantee you do not do whatever you multi-task the best that you could. If something is worth doing, it's worth doing well! Perhaps you multi-task because you forget how important accelerated learning is to your life. Well, then you need to take inventory of your life right now to remember what is important to you and why. If the accelerated learning process is not your priority, then what are you doing? To be happy, you need to be clear about what you are doing with your time and your life. What is a mistake? It is anything that took you in a direction you didn't want to go.

Sometimes when a person gets lost, they discover new frontiers or a new way to get home. There are always new discoveries to be found in our so-called mistakes. Instead of getting down on yourself, make sure you take advantage of all the learning opportunities that your mistakes always provide you.

11.2

So, get ready to make a lot of mistakes! Are you ready to mess up and fail? Good, because if you are, you're ready to truly accelerate your learning. Of course, our goal is always to succeed. We are striving for perfection even if we know we can't ever get there. The intention to be as perfect as possible is what will drive us to more perfection than if we didn't care. Sometimes, though, we put so much pressure on ourselves to be perfect that we can't help but make a mistake. The truth is there is no such thing as perfect. Perfect is so subjective. There is no one standard for everyone. So, just do the best you can and relax if that means you make a few mistakes. You will always learn more from your mistakes than you ever will from being as perfect as you can be.

Sometimes mistakes are not so obvious. Well, in those cases, it's important to use your intuition. Other times when we're not sure, others will let us know that we made a mistake. All industries have a professional standard that an amateur will not always be able to live up to until she has practiced and studied like an expert. Anything that makes you suffer is trying to teach you something.

No one should have to suffer unnecessarily, so do not hesitate to consult with a mentor about a difficult situation that you face. Or do some research to see what others more knowledgeable than you have to say about it. Even experts have to do their research and consult with a mentor or colleague. Other students like you can also prove to be invaluable when it comes to advising. You are not required to follow any of the advice that you receive, but it certainly gives you much to think about. When you seek out your answer, this gives you a measure of control over your problem that you didn't have before. Even if you don't choose to make any changes, that is your choice, and somehow the pain of suffering doesn't hurt quite as much.

"If you live long enough, you'll make mistakes. But if you learn from them, you'll be a better person." – Bill Clinton

---

Observe any baby or kid learn something new. Before they ever learn how to do something right, they do it all wrong again and again. This is the pattern of learning when you're a human. Just because we're all grown up doesn't mean that we always know how to do everything. Compared to what we already know, there so many more things that we do not know. This is something that we need to accept as being a part of the human condition. So, like a kid, take pride in all the mistakes that you have to make whenever you learn something new. The great thing about being a kid is that nobody expects you to know anything. That takes so much of the pressure off, doesn't it? As adults in this society, we need to re-examine our attitudes about learning. All of us have something to learn, no matter what our age or experience level. Anyone who does not have anything to learn is dead. It's as simple as that. The more we learn, the more mistakes we have to make.

11.3

Be organized.

Do your research.

Be prepared.

Take care of your health and your environment to maximize your learning potential.

If this is what you do for yourself, you are prepared for any mistake that you make… or that anyone else makes. You are human, and humans have to make mistakes in order to learn. How much more true this is when you commit yourself to accelerating your learning process. So, take care of yourself and your life. If you are in school, make sure you stay on top of your schedule and are early for all of your classes. Do all your homework and study the hours that it takes to get an A. Doing so will give you confidence and prepare you for anything. All of us are students, but those of us who are learning for the sheer joy of it, not because we are in a class, we especially need to take care of ourselves and our schedule. No one else is telling us to go into our learning space to learn. That is our idea.

The biggest mistake that you can make in this situation is to not follow through on what it is that you want to do. You want to be fluent in Russian by January 1st. Okay, maybe that was a lot to take on. Maybe you were a little too ambitious with your goal. Congratulate yourself for being so ambitious! This is a wonderful quality. Not many people have the drive to want to be fluent in such a difficult language as Russian. But you can do it if you put together a plan. Perhaps it is more realistic to aim to be able to conduct a successful conversation in Russian with a native speaker by January 1st. See, you didn't really make a mistake at all!

You were always on your way to doing just that... you just didn't know it, yet. "If you shut your door to all errors, truth will be shut out." – Rabindranath Tagore

---

Make sure you don't waste the incredible learning opportunity that your mistakes offer you. Mistakes were not meant to be swept under the rug. Make sure you make the best use of them. Be absolutely determined to turn all your mistakes into the greatest discoveries in your learning process. Mistakes are always diamonds in the rough and hidden golden nuggets. The truth in disguise. How do we tap into the power of mistakes? By taking action. Even if our action does not immediately unlock the answer, the act of getting into action, at the very least, begins the process. If one action doesn't achieve your goal, try something new. If you don't know what to do next, just do anything. Any action will activate your brain to find its own answer.

Your Quick Start Action Step:

What is a mistake that you made? Take out your journal and write out what happened. Write it out just the way that you have always viewed this mistake. Now, turn it around and write about what this mistake taught you and how it changed your thinking. Was it really a mistake? If it took you to a new level you never had achieved before, perhaps it was a portal to new information you wouldn't have ever encountered any other way. Or was it a mistake? Explain why. Give it a day and return back to what you wrote and think about it. Consider this to be a crucial part of your accelerated learning process!

Bonus Chapter: Go-To Learning Strategies to Prepare for an Exam

○ ○

A B C

D E F

✓ ± ×

Bonus Chapter: Go-To Learning Strategies to Prepare for an Exam

12.1

This book has prepared you with all that you need to know to prepare for an exam. You need to have a learning space conducive to study. You need to take care of your health by eating a variety of organic vegetables combined with protein and fat. Your brain needs the increased blood flow that comes from regular physical exercise. You also need to make sure that you are a student who is always studying and not leaving it all for the night before your test.

You might pass your exam if you cram, but if you want to accelerate your learning process, cramming is never going to get you there. When you cram, you don't remember very much at all in the long run. So, take pride in being a professional student and use this book to do it better than you ever have before. All semester you should be preparing for your midterm and final exam. It doesn't start a month or two weeks before the date of your exam. Your preparation begins on the first day of class. Always stay ahead of all the reading you have to do, if you can, and do all homework assignments.

You will want to always be going back over your detailed notes, and you might even want to rewrite and re-organize your notes, so they make sense to your own particular style of learning. You can never over-exposeyourself to the class material, so record your classes if your instructor allows you to so you can listen to them more than once. The more ways you can go over the information on your test, the more deeply it will all be embedded into your brain.

A good way to know where you stand with the information is to create your own exam and test yourself. In the process of creating such an exam, you will learn a lot more of the information that you expect. Many students make their own study guides. Again, the process of making your own study guide does wonder to help you retain the information that you learn. If you don't have the time to make your own study guide, there is a website that posts the study guides of other students who have taken your class. Just google your class number and school followed by the word, "quizlet," and if there are any study guides posted, they will come up.

It is best for your accelerated learning process to create your own study guide geared towards your own brain, but it is very helpful to have a website like this when you find yourself running out of time. Another trick is to chew a certain brand and flavor of gum while you study and then chew this same brand and flavor of gum when you take your exam. Flavor and smell are one of the most powerful memory aids for our brain. Studying while listening to classical music is also a way that you can help your brain process complex information. There is a lot of complexity in classical music that seems to supercharge the complexity of the brain.

12.2

When it comes time to take your exam, it's very important to stay calm and relaxed. If you have been doing the work to prepare yourself all semester, the exam is nothing other than review for you. You've got this! Know what to expect on the exam. Is it open book or open note? If it is, make sure that you have put together everything you need the night before. The more prepared you are, the calmer you will be. If you are faced with true/false questions, be sure to read the question very carefully as well as the wording of the instructions.

It's when you haven't carefully read the instructions that you can make the simplest mistakes on such questions, even if you know the right answer. A lot of the time the answer to multiple choice questions is, "All of the above," but make sure you carefully read the wording of the question, so you don't make an unnecessary mistake. When an answer is rather long, it many times is the correct answer. If the exam is standardized, there should be an equal number of A, B and C answers. Read all questions very carefully and cross out all the wrong answers if you are able to in order to lower the chances of you accidentally selecting the wrong answer. Whenever there is an "always" or "never" or "not" – be careful. Such answers can trick you into selecting the wrong answer if you don't read them carefully. If it is an essay exam, make sure you plan what you want to write before you start writing.

Keep in mind that your instructor will be looking for the standard introduction, body, and conclusion. Make sure you have read the question carefully and fully restate it at the beginning of your answer. Completely answer the question asked. Be sure to review your answers before turning in your test, but always go with your first answer unless you catch something that you missed in the question or you have uncovered new proof that your first answer was wrong. Make sure you have answered all questions unless you don't know the answer and you are penalized more for wrong answers than those that you skip. If you have taken the time to prepare, an exam should be an exciting opportunity to prove this to your instructor.

You have already put yourself to the test on your own, and now you are making it official. Take pride in all the work that you did to be able to prove the mastery of your course material. Congratulations!

12.3

The most important thing that you can go through in preparation for an exam is your notes. Focus on the area of the material that you are weakest. Go over your study guide at least 5-7 days in advance of your test. When it comes to history and science, make sure you have extra paper to write down more explanation of anything you're less sure of. Check off all that you know on your study guide. Keep going over your study guide again and again until everything is checked off.

As for math and chemistry, the study guides you get from your teacher will probably be a set of questions. Do all the problems and any that you can't figure out, ask your teacher or other students for help. Such study guides will usually prepare you enough for your exams. Quizlet.com is the best for last minute reviewing the day before the final. This is really good for information-based classes such as biology or psychology.

Search for chapters and different topics, and you'll find many terms listed that you can go over. I didn't mention it, but flash cards are absolutely essential. You should be using them all semester for all the terms and other information that you need to learn. You can take flashcards anywhere which is so very convenient. There are plenty of flashcard websites out there where you can print them up if you don't want to make your own. But there is a lot to be said for making your own. Use colors and have fun with them! It's impossible to go over your entire textbook before an exam, but your textbook is very helpful for review of certain areas you're not as clear on. The chapter reviews at the end of every chapter can save you a lot of time and help you see what you need to work on. Practice putting concepts into your own words. If you can't do this, you don't understand the concept and need to work on it.

To remember more at the exam, review everything the night before just before bedtime. If you go over everything that will be on the exam, your brain will work on it overnight, and you will remember so much of what you reviewed when you wake up. Make sure you get plenty of sleep instead of staying up all night studying for your exam. If you have no other choice but to cram, make sure you do this a day in advance, so you get a full night's rest the night before the exam.

Before you go to sleep, merely review everything so that your subconscious mind can unlock the information for you. Mind mapping is also very helpful when preparing for an exam. Everyone's mind map is unique. You start with a concept, and you might draw a circle around it, then you draw a line to connect it to another "bubble" containing another concept, details or explanation.

Mind maps mimic the way that our brain thinks and really put on paper what our thoughts look like. This is such a great way to prepare for an exam. Any gaps in your understanding are on paper for you to see. When it's time to prepare for finals, you must create a study schedule. The whole purpose of this schedule is to get you away from your tendency to procrastinate, help you focus on the most crucial material to study and help you stay healthy and as stress-free as possible. Make sure you know when and where each and every one of your finals are. You also need to know the format of all your exams (true / false, multiple choice or essay?), how much each of your exams will count towards your final grade for the course, if each of your exams will merely cover the latest chapter or be a review of all that you've learned all semester.

As you prepare for your finals, you also have to make sure that you are aware of what homework assignments you are responsible for turning in during the final week. And how do you like to work? Do you like to alternate studying with doing your homework projects in one day or do you like to focus on one or the other for one day at a time? Make sure you have all your syllabi, course materials and handouts for each class as well as all notes, textbooks and study guides. At this point, #1 priority is evaluating your command of knowledge in each class.

What will be covered on each of your finals and where are you weakest? Which classes are the most important, which classes do you have the most work to do and which order would you like to do this work in? There are going to be some finals that count more towards your final grade so you will need to make sure you allow more time to study for them. You also might not have to spend as much time preparing for finals in classes that you already have a solid A in. Focus on your weaknesses. Just before finals, you need to put everything on your schedule... meals, errands – everything that you have to do every day. Try to group all your non-study activities together so that you have as many uninterrupted big blocks of time available for preparing for your finals. Google calendar is great, but use whatever works for you. Color code your exam dates, class times, work, your study times, homework, errands, meals, workouts, social outings, etc. so that you will know what to do at a glance.

Scheduling different things every 30 minutes can help you vary your work and energy. When scheduling, it's also a good idea to keep in mind when your energy levels at their highest and lowest.

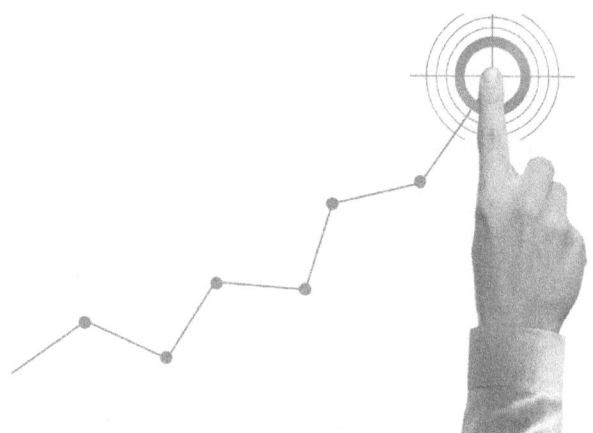

Don't forget to schedule in breaks, exercise, and meals. This is the time that you must keep your body in mind together! If you get too overwhelmed, do not be afraid to ask for help from friends, other students or your instructor. Knowing your instructor's office hours can be so very helpful for times like this when you might need their assistance.

Your Quick Start Action Step:

Pick a study technique from this chapter and check it out. Try a certain brand and flavor of gum to chew while studying and then also chew it during your exam. Did you remember more? Get some index cards and have fun creating your own flashcards for a topic that you're learning. Go to Quizlet.com and see what you can find there. What did you choose to try? Did it help? Continue applying what you've learned until it becomes second nature to you.

Conclusion

Thank you again for owning this book! I hope this book was able to help you to accelerate your learning in ways that you didn't expect. The next step is to read this book again and implement all the ideas that you'd like to try.

Thank you and good luck!

www.ingramcontent.com/pod-product-compliance
Lightning Source LLC
Chambersburg PA
CBHW071238070526
44583CB00017B/2230